# STEPS TO FIRST-CLASS RUGGER

*Swinging Through the Gap*

# STEPS TO
# FIRST-CLASS RUGGER

BY

GEOFFREY DE LA CONDAMINE

WITH A FOREWORD BY

SIR WAVELL WAKEFIELD, M.P.

*President of the Rugby Union*
*(Cambridge & England)*

LONDON : HERBERT JENKINS

*First published by*
*Herbert Jenkins Ltd.*
*3, Duke of York Street,*
*London, S.W.1.*
1950

PRINTED AND BOUND IN GREAT BRITAIN BY WILLIAM CLOWES AND SONS, LIMITED
LONDON AND BECCLES

# ACKNOWLEDGMENTS

MY thanks are due to John Stapleton Harris and Malcolm McNeill for some brilliant photography, to M. V. D. and P. J. G. for invaluable help, to my Skipper and to the boys who appeared in the pictures. I have also to acknowledge the assistance of the members of the Oxford University Rugby Football Club who so willingly co-operated to provide three of the action photographs.

G. DE LA C.

*Guernsey.*

# FOREWORD

BY SIR WAVELL WAKEFIELD, M.P.

*President of the Rugby Union*
*(Cambridge and England)*

THE author of this book has been a Rugby football coach at a junior school for fifteen years. Five of those years were spent in learning what was required of him and developing his methods. In his schooldays he was in the Sherborne XV, and at eighteen was playing for the Harlequins. He gained a Freshers and a final trial at Oxford, but at the beginning of his last year damaged a knee and never played again. The first results of his teaching are now showing on the playing fields. One of the earliest of the boys he taught secured a Blue at Oxford; another, at the age of sixteen, has just played for his county, a third for the Navy. One of his boys has captained Stowe, another Radley. Since the end of the war six of the boys that he trained as juniors have played for the Harlequins First XV.

The author had two intentions when he conceived this book.

First, to prove by means of a camera, and beyond all shadow of doubt, that boys from the age of thirteen upwards, with proper coaching and unremitting care, are capable of playing a first-class game in miniature, that they can go through the same technical movements and do the same things as are expected in the higher class "Rugger", and do them with the same rhythm and polish.

He argued that there was no reason why forwards should not be as skilful in tackling, heeling, and wheeling, why his scrum-half should not throw proportionately as accurate a pass, his fly-half and the three-quarters should not jink, dummy, and cut inside, the wings swerve and cross-kick, and his full-back catch and kick as well, technically, as any player in a first-class side. That he is right is shown by the photographs in this book.

Second, to show that, if his boys could reach such a standard, there was no reason why hundreds of other boys should not do the same, and so raise the standard of Rugby football to its pre-war level.

To do this coaches must know their job and be able to carry it out with patience and precision and, above all, a deep knowledge of the science of the game. They must know just where the scrum-half should put his feet and his weight in order to deliver the proper pass.

They must be able to teach a hooker how to swing for the ball instead of vaguely sticking out a leg. They must know the true value of a quick change in the direction of attack, so often dependent on a real and understood control of speed.

In fact, all coaches, whatever standard of play they themselves attained, must be thoroughly knowledgeable in every phase of the game.

So the author has summarised his own coaching methods in the hope that they will help others and serve as a sound basis on which they can build their own individual methods of coaching.

In addition to the technical photographs there are plates of several movements that will be of great interest to students of the game.

One, *Operation "Shorts"*, is based on the short American pass and camouflage of the scrum; the other, on the change in direction of attack based on a reverse pass.

There is also a formation for loose heeling called the *Fan* and the *Offensive Fall*, invented to offset the weakness of distributed weight.

There is an *Operation "Ginger"* that opens the way for a breakaway by the scrum-half. There is also a *magnetic blackboard* on which these tactics can be explained.

All these operations, whether successful or not, have the merit of attempting to change the direction of attack, which is essential in modern football. It is in this way that situations are created to disorganise the defence and prepare the way for the most favourable conditions for attack. For Rugby football is essentially a game of ATTACK, and in this book even tackling and falling are based on this simple and elemental truth.

Much has been written about Rugby football in the past and, no doubt, much will be written in the future. This book is a valuable contribution to what has been written previously because the approach has been from a fresh angle. The author has made a thorough study of the game and is not afraid to try out ideas. The results achieved show that, through his own knowledge and enthusiasm, he has taught his boys not only to understand the game but, above all, to have confidence in themselves and a real love for our great game.

The record of matches won is impressive. But far more important than the mere winning of matches is the impression made on the boys. Here indeed is shown that, by practice and an infinite capacity for taking trouble, the best can be achieved when the teaching is right.

I firmly believe that, if boys realise how much greater is the enjoyment and fun obtained from playing Rugby football if thought is given to the game and trouble is taken diligently to practise passing, dribbling, and kicking, together with a variety of combined movements, and that skill in achievement does not come easily, then greater effort will be made by coaches and boys to improve their knowledge and skill.

This book should do much to further this end.   But let coaches never forget, and boys always remember, that, far more important than the winning of matches and the skilful execution of movements, is that indefinable spirit of the game which must be for ever nurtured in the hearts of the young so that they, in their turn, can carry on untarnished the glorious traditions of the game handed down to us by our fathers.

# CONTENTS

# ILLUSTRATIONS

# STEPS TO
# FIRST-CLASS RUGGER

# OBJECTS OF THE BOOK

I CHOSE the title *STEPS TO FIRST-CLASS RUGGER* because I have learnt by results that the seeds of first-class rugger can, by intelligent coaching, be implanted in a boy while he is still in his early teens. Moreover, it is possible for a team of youngsters to play first-class Rugger in miniature.

The first of these statements can only be proved by those whom I have had the honour to coach and to whom I dedicate this book.

The second is more fallible in one way and more easily proved in the other. The photographs in this book will clearly show that boys of thirteen can go through the same actions as their elder brethren who are playing for their clubs, counties, or countries.

Some weeks ago I came across my full-back who was looking with envious eyes at a picture of G. A. Hollis kicking a ball, in a book called *Do It This Way*, produced by Mark Sugden and Hollis himself. The boy said to me somewhat wistfully, "Do you think I will be able to kick like that when I am his age?"

I suggested that he could do just as well now, and in order to substantiate my statement I took a photograph of him which proved to his entire satisfaction and with no little increase to his morale, that there was no difference at all in his technique. Those who have that book might be interested in comparing the right-footed kick of an eminent England player with that of Master X, the full-back in Plate 78.

I would like every boy who reads this book to realise that he can do all that he sees in other books festooned with pictures of Internationals and other great men.

To those responsible for coaching I have tried to explain my methods, born of fifteen years' trial, error, and argument, as clearly and concisely as possible. The photographs, luckily, speak for themselves, and I have merely added the necessary technical comments. But I would like my adult readers to remember that the tactics described in this book are primarily for sides up to sixteen years of age, which explains the absence of stress upon such forms of attack as all types of "scissors" and particularly the cross-kick. I consider these to be suitable to more mature players. The latter, always a feature of Welsh club sides, was used to considerable effect by Cambridge in the 1948 'Varsity match, though there was no youthful W. W. Wakefield up to clinch matters.   It nevertheless remains a most potent match winner if used with discretion and skill.

I hope with the combination of coaching and photographs that those in charge of young Rugger at schools may benefit, and that the boys themselves may realise their own natural potentialities.

# THE FORWARDS

*Ingredients:* Eight boys who are willing to mix it and to give and take punishment. That necessitates courage, physique, and a considerable amount of personal aggression.

Having selected your eight, proceed to size them for the tight scrums. I have found it preferable to have a big front row, with the exception of the hooker, who can over- or underpack as the occasion demands. The second row will supply the weight; therefore as a rule place your two biggest and tallest boys there, providing they are much of a size.

Lock-forward or middle of the back row is generally reserved for one of the less skilful brethren, as it is the easiest place in which to pack, but the lightest and most agile of your eight are more likely to fill the wing forward positions.

Early in the season do not worry too much about the packing in the tight, or even such simple things as the first shove, but generally concentrate on these points: (*a*) to develop a controlled ferocity in the loose; (*b*) to keep foremost in your mind of ATTACK at all times; (*c*) to understand the principle of foot over and the reason why the speed with which this is done is of paramount importance; (*d*) to learn to listen to the leader of the pack and to obey at once; and finally (*e*) to be on or near the ball the whole game.

When these points are sufficiently drilled home and partially mastered, the leader may be placed in the position of scrum-half for a quarter of an hour or so against the stronger pack. He will then find out by rueful personal experience that his forwards must also *bind and shove* when they loose heel, otherwise the enemy pack come through and much damage is done both to morale and fingers.

From this moment the "*Fan*" formation is adopted in loose heeling and the scrum-half begins to get a little more protection.

By this time the forwards have begun to settle down and attention must turn progressively from the hooker, who must be taught to swing for the ball, to the binding of the front row, to the second row's feet (somehow they always seem to be twice as big as anyone else's), and finally to the back row and the functions of the wing forwards.

At this stage of training the "whistle game" should be much in evidence. When the whistle blows the players freeze just where they are, and they have an opportunity to see which of them are where they ought to be. The coach also has a general survey and probably delivers a homily suitably couched to those who are out of position. The players are then reset, the whistle is blown, and the game goes on from where it had stopped. This is a particularly valuable form of training for positioning, and also for lazy forwards who are inclined to be trapped twenty yards from the ball with no forthcoming excuse, a fault that might well pass unnoticed in a game.

The next step is the start of match play, the coach's final guide to his pack, for many a boy is a lion amongst his own fellows and a veritable sheep among boys of another XV.

If necessary the final shake-out is made, after which the forwards should start to consider themselves as a *pack*. Dribbling practice, which consists of weaving the ball between flags set at a distance narrowed down as the season advances, is instituted, and line-out work is begun. The wheel and straight shove are tried, the long pass from the enemy kick-off, and various niceties of forward play that are fun for the pack to try and a reward for continued hard work; but in the midst of these polishing activities the pack must never forget their real job, that of *engaging*, *defeating*, and finally completely *dominating*, any other pack that they meet.

It cannot be too strongly stressed that without this domination the threequarters are unable to function as they should, and if every one of the eight forwards goes on the field with this primary object in view it is amazing how time and again they will eventually, perhaps only by better morale and a clearer idea of their job, defeat an enemy pack of the same size and skill. If their leader knows his job, they will play full out for the whole game without the need for any additional encouragement from the touchline.

## PACKING

FRONT ROW

Bind tight, knees slightly bent, shove inwards towards hooker, straighten necks when in, which helps to make backs straight.

SECOND ROW

Bind before going down, get in at the level of the front row's knees, then by straightening the neck work up till the shoulders are shoving the buttocks of the front row. Backs straight, bind tight. The ball should be visible in the front row to both second-row forwards.

*Either* inside feet up *or* outside in order to make a tunnel, but both must do the same. Shove slightly inwards.

It is most important to get in at knee level, for if the second-row forwards try to force their heads in at the level of the buttocks they will be shoving downwards and crumpling the front row and the hooker.

Lock-forward or middle of the back, same drill as second row except that he shoves straight off *both* feet, leaving a space between them as the finish of the tunnel made by second-row feet.

Wing forwards in last and shoving slightly *inwards* on to the second row. They bind lock-forward, but he binds on to second row only, in order to keep wing forwards mobile.

These positions are, of course, ideal, and nobody will get forwards to pack exactly in this way. But once they have got into the drill, a little shifting of legs and weight will ensure comfort, which is all-important in packing, without losing the essential direction of the shove and the conception of the "tunnel".

\*     \*     \*

*Plate 1*

Plates 1 and 2 show two ways in which the hooker can bind. In Plate 1 the White hooker is underpacking, his arms being under those of the two flank men. Note that the binding is tight, the hips being drawn together. This is of great importance, for if the binding is loose the front row will be split by the second row when they come in.

*Plate 2*

Overpacking. Possibly a better grip, but as usual comfort and size decide which shall be used.

*Plate 3*

This shows the second row now in, with the ball in position of the middle of the tunnel. This is by no means an ideal picture, for though both second-row forwards are shoving inwards as they should and both have their inside feet up, the right-hand man has not got his back straight enough and therefore is somewhat lopsided.

26

*Plate 4*

This shows the whole scrum and the end of the tunnel with the ball coming out between the lock-forward's feet. Lock-forward has got his feet nicely apart, but the right foot should be in advance so as to maintain his shove. At present he is just leaning on the second row. Blind side wing-forward was just settling into position as the shot was taken. His right hand should be binding lock-forward.

# HOOKING

*Plate 5*

The scrum-half has put his ball in on the open head side; White hooker, whose left leg was placed *back* and *slightly behind* his right, has swung for the ball and got it clear in the middle of his *right* or *hooking foot*. This swing is of great importance and can only be properly timed if the scrum-half stands as he is, at a proper distance from the scrum, holds the ball with one point in each, and then goes through this drill: "On your *right* (or *left*) Whites, coming in, *now*." The first remark is cautionary; the last three words make it possible for the hooker to time his swing, the ball being released by the scrum-half at the last word and aimed to meet his hooker's swinging foot on the *half-volley*. Should all this be done accurately, provided that the rest of the pack straighten their bent knees at the word "*now*" (sometimes referred to as the First Shove), his swing should beat his opposite number every time that it is his own side's ball. The scrum-half, of course, will put the ball in *always* on his loose head side. Obviously much practice between scrum-half and front row is necessary.

In this plate the binding of White front row is not tight enough, the left-hand man being at fault.

*Plate 6*

This shows the same procedure, save here the binding is good and the enemy have not come through. The outside men are shoving inwards and have straightened their knees correctly. *Black* loose head can be clearly seen on the right of the plate.

Next to the half-backs and the hooker I would place in importance the *open-side wing forward*. (For the purposes of this book I have taken the open side to mean the side farthest away from the touchline, and the blind side to be the side nearest to the touchline.) Like them he is a specialist, and like them also has to have special instruction and, if possible, to possess certain peculiar attributes that are not necessary for the rest of the pack.

The open-side forward should remain in that position for the whole of the game once he has learnt his job and knows something of the technique of the rest of the back row, irrespective of where the play is. There are schools, and even first-class clubs, which play their wing forwards left and right, and not open and blind. There is no sense in this, as the virtues of the open-side wing forward, and indeed his training, are so totally different from those of his blind-side comrade.

His job is dual. First in attack, to be up at the most favourable place for a pass when his threequarters are on the move, and secondly in defence, to be, *par excellence*, the blotter-out of the fly-half, and thus the early spoiler of enemy movements.

Let us take his attacking duties first: if his side secures the ball and heels, he will be the nearest mobile player *inside* the fly-half, and so his first job is to be up with him in case of a break and the possibility of an *inside* pass. Secondly, he will have an admirable cross view of his own attack, and will be able to see how and where this is developing. This gives him the unique oportunity of being able to anticipate, with some accuracy, where he is most likely to be of use. In time he will get to know the favourite tactics of his halves and centres and thus be able to use his mobility to the full. Indeed, in attack his keyword is *anticipation*, and he must never forget it. One cannot teach it, one can merely point it out incessantly and underline it if one is lucky by astute use of the whistle in the "whistle game". He must also be reasonably adept at the giving and taking of a pass, so he should frequently be included among the backs in their passing practice. On wet days, when the threequarters are likely to drop or fumble their passes, it is good tactics for the wing forward to follow the course of the ball behind the threequarters. It is possible for him to do this because of the slowing down of the tempo; it is useful because the inside pass is less likely, and in the event of any breakdown in the passing, not allowed for or permitted on a dry day, he will be in position to take the ball on with his feet, or even pick it up and try again. So much for his normal attacking duties.

In defence his first and foremost duty is to see that the enemy fly-half does not break through. To ensure this he must learn *against his own natural tendency* not to run *at* the fly-half but *across* his intended path.

If, as many wing forwards do, he goes *for* the fly-half, that player, owing to the high speed which his opponent must use to get in a tackling position, will have ample opportunity of slipping inside him, probably creating a formidable gap in the defence of a junior side. Should he follow the former method, he will, of necessity, drive the fly-half across the ground, and may be able to use this *MAXIMUM CONTROLLED EFFICIENT SPEED* either to tackle him in his own time or to cause a jerked and hasty pass.

It is my contention that the open-side wing forward will seldom be able to lay a hand on a fly-half who knows his job and passes the ball on to his centre in three to five paces, aided, of course, with an efficient service from the base of the scrum, but he can blot out his personal attack, drive him across the field, and, as I have said, if these ideal conditions are not fulfilled, can even tackle him in possession.

This technique cannot be emphasised too strongly, as my experience is that all young wing forwards will try to attack the fly-half by running directly at him instead of cutting him off, at his own selected spot.

So the forward to fill this position must be fastish and intelligent, the operative word being "intelligent".

*The blind-side wing forward* is the next in order of precedence and in training. To him lies the task of dealing with the scrum-half. Ball lost, head up, round the base of the scrum to harass or, if the heel is not clear or the player slow, to spoil him in possession. For the rest I leave him a roving commission.

The *lock-forward* or middle of the back row. This player's attacking activities are limited if he is doing his job in the tight scrums—and most important it is—of giving the final and straightest shove right up to the last moment until the ball is out and away. When this has been accomplished, his head comes up, he disengages, and follows the open-side wing forward, but inside his path.

Should the enemy scrum-half break away on his own from a tight scrum, it is his unenviable job to get up quickly and block it, leaving the open-side wing forward to shadow the fly-half. My own opinion as to this possibility has been expressed in the section dealing with the scrum-half.

*       *       *

In the section on forwards my third point (*c*) was "to understand the principle of foot over and the reason why the speed with which this is done is of paramount importance".

Those two last words were carefully weighed, for if any one operation can be said to win or lose matches more than another it is the control of the ball in the loose. It is far more important to have the ball coming constantly back from the loose mauls than it is to have mastery over the tight scrums.

The reason is obvious. In the tight the enemy's defence line is carefully positioned and ready for the attack. Each defender knows that if the ball is heeled by the other side an attack will develop, and unless some unorthodox movement is used they know the direction from which this attack will come. It is therefore difficult to penetrate a line of an aware defence in these circumstances.

Not so when the ball comes back quickly from a loose maul. The all-important word is *quickly*. The defence is not so perfectly positioned, indeed there may well be gaps in it; defenders may be off balance and uncertain from where the attack is coming. It is the perfect opportunity for the threequarters to show their tricks and their paces, and there are no wing forwards to help to block and destroy the attack. But all these splendid things only happen if that ball comes back from the loose in a flash and is whipped away by the scrum-half.

After much thought I conceived and adopted two methods which help to obtain this vital speed. I had observed that time and again the ball was heeled slowly after a forward attack because of the difficulty of hooking over the body of the opponent who had stopped the rush. It occurred to me how satisfying it would be if one of my own side had fallen on the ball, thus creating a bulwark from which to heel instead of an obstacle which must first be pulled aside or stepped over before the ball came out. I decided to experiment on these lines and from these experiments the *Offensive Fall* was born.

At the moment when it became obvious that our forward attack was going to be stopped, the pack leader called for an offensive fall. The nearest man on our side dropped on the ball, thus deliberately stopping the attack, the forwards gathered round, and the ball was heeled, and very quickly too.

I had also observed that the scrum-half often suffered in the loose from inadequate protection, gaps being left in the scrum through which a hostile body, or even an arm or leg, could stop the ball being passed out. These gaps generally occurred because the forwards were inclined to pack on each other opposite the ball. This created a narrow frontage and certainly more than one pair of legs were between the ball and the scrum-half.

To surmount this difficulty a *"Fan" Formation* was adopted, the name being derived from the fact that the forwards fan out and shove inwards, the procedure being thus:

### OFFENSIVE FALL

First man down on the ball, the next nearest the ball prepared to heel, the next two binding on each side of him, the remainder of the pack to come in on either flank, being particularly careful to leave only one pair of legs between the ball and the scrum-half. Those on the flanks to pack shoving inwards, in this way making the *"Fan" Formation*.

Ideally the shape gives protection to the scrum-half, at the same time ensuring that the ball is heeled with the greatest possible speed.

These methods were given a prolonged trial, and they proved so successful that they have taken precedence of third place in the training of forwards. There were, of course, and still are, snags, perhaps the most frequent being the ill-timing of the offensive fall, but the ball does come back so constantly and fast that it has enabled the threequarters to keep up an attacking pressure that has proved fatal to our opponents.

For those who are interested in the rules of the game I might add that I took the highest technical advice, a member of the Committee of the R.U., as to whether or no the *Offensive Fall* created any kind of obstruction by which a side could be penalised. The answer was an emphatic *no*, and I must admit that no referee up to the present moment has taken exception to it.

All packs must try to make their loose heeling as scientific as possible. In order to do this they must concentrate on it early in the season and keep ever in mind the necessity of speed of heeling and protection for the scrum-half. Once the pack realise the importance of both these conditions the threequarters will be given the chance to attack for most of the game, which should mean victory.

\*　　　\*　　　\*

3

# THE "FAN" FORMATION

Three plates show this formation for loose heeling, which has already been described.

\* \* \*

*Plate 7*

A ground shot. The ball has just been heeled and the scrum-half, comfortably ensconced in the angle of the fan, is about to pass the ball out. It will be noticed that the scrum-half is correctly standing sideways on to the scrum and *not directly square to it*. In this position he is already half-facing his fly-half. Had he been square on, an elementary mistake that young players often make, he would have had to turn with the ball, thus making two movements instead of one.

\* \* \*

*Plate 8*

An aerial view. This time there are some criticisms, though the shape of the formation can be clearly seen. The right-hand White forward has been slow in coming up, and has not had time to bind before the shot was taken. The left-hand forward who forms the horn of the fan could have been better advised to pack one place to his right, thereby making more use of his weight without spoiling the formation. It is obvious from this plate how essential to the fan formation is the speed with which the ball is heeled. Should it stick, Black pack should be able to brush through the protective screen, as their weight is more concentrated. Hence the necessity of the *Offensive Fall* to obviate this difficulty. Black threequarter line is coming up to deal with the heel. Note the position of White scrum-half's right foot. It is rightly placed, the weight being behind the ball, so that the pass will not be "ballooned".

*Plate 9*

The final phase. Black scrum-half has been unable to interfere, and a nice long pass is coming out to the fly-half. If anything, perhaps White scrum-half is a trifle too low to get the full benefit of the follow-through. It will be noticed that he has not cast himself on to his stomach—a point referred to at considerable length in the section on the ideal passing of a scrum-half.

\*          \*          \*

# THE WHEEL

A movement rarely seen nowadays, but effective if it is done with speed. There has always been some controversy as to its use. Originally its value was to relieve pressure of attack on or near one's own line, but owing to the intricacy of the technique and the possibilities of losing possession, I am doubtful as to its defensive value. Personally I am more inclined to the heel back in order to allow either half to find touch. But I have found that as an *ATTACKING* measure it is most useful, especially as a variation of tactics.

Its success depends on the speed of the operation, and also on its surprise value. Hence a code word must be used in order to keep the enemy unaware till the last possible moment. Should it be stopped, as it can be, by an astute scrum-half or blind-side wing forward, there is still a chance of a quick loose heel and an attack, started on the *same* side as the wheel, for the threequarters, unhampered by enemy forwards who will be out of position, may combine with some success. The fly-half, his threequarters following him, gets up close on the same side as the wheel as soon as the ball is secured, in order to be in position to take a short pass from his partner if the wheel is checked.

The blocking of this manœuvre is simple, for if spotted by the opposition in time a quick fall will result in a chaos of bodies, and probably the formation of another tight scrum by order of the referee, unless the quick loose heel that I have already mentioned is successful.

The procedure of the wheel is as follows. The ball is heeled and held in the second row. The scrum is swung to either flank depending on loose head. This swing is made possible by the left-hand front-row man shoving hard and *inwards* and the hooker and the right-hand front-row man forcing their way *backwards*, or *vice versa*. Thus the second row, who have the ball, are helped to disengage. The front row continue to shove for all they are worth in order to avoid being pushed off the ball before it is out on the wheel. This also keeps the enemy pack engaged.

\*        \*        \*

# THE WHEEL

*Plates 10 and 11*

These show two action photographs of the wheel, the first, wheeling towards the left flank; the second, towards the right.

In both cases the preliminary procedure, that of heeling, holding, and wheeling the scrum, has already taken place. The White front rows are still shoving *hard*, to hold up the Black packs. The second-row forward has the ball at his feet, his partner being half concealed behind him, and he is being directly supported by the wing forward; lock-forward in both cases is coming up as well. The Black wing forward who might have held up the rush is particularly at fault in Plate 10, and in Plate 11 has got his head up far too late to deal with the movement. White fly-half can be seen in the same plate coming across into position for the possible short pass from the scrum-half mentioned before, if the wheel is held up.

It will be noticed that the ball is being watched most closely by all the forwards concerned and that those actually dribbling it have their heads well over, very necessary if control is to be kept.

The position of the halfway line in Plate 11 shows both the angle of the wheel and the attacking nature of the operation.

A most useful way of initiating a threequarter attack, as they have the complete width of the field in which to manœuvre and the wing forwards are at a distinct discount if the scrum-half has a reasonably long pass.

One seldom sees it done cleanly nowadays, save perhaps by overseas touring sides, which seems a pity.

The movement necessitates an accurate throw by the wing and accurate timing of the leap.   To ensure complete success it also needs a forward who has mastered the *turn in the air* while timing his jump, in the same way as B. H. Black and W. E. Henley, the Oxford Blues, used to do.

The following six plates show the process of delivering the ball to the scrum-half, and of the scrum-half passing it out to his fly-half.

*      *      *

*Plate 12*

Preliminary positions.   The wing has the ball nicely balanced and is judging the distance of his throw to White forward No. 5.   To get the ball at the correct height for No. 5 to catch he will actually aim at No. 6. The No. 1 White forward has very properly turned inwards, as he knows that the ball will comfortably clear him, and he is in a position to get more quickly to the focal point if anything should go wrong.   It is interesting to note that many arms are raised for no reason, but the expert has contented himself by getting on his toes.

*      *      *

*Plate 13*

The wing has thrown accurately.   No. 5 has leapt, *turned in mid-air*, and made his catch.   No. 1 is coming round quickly to help form a loose scrum if necessary.

*      *      *

*Plate 14*

The scrum-half is in the act of receiving and has cradled his arms nicely. It will be seen that he is about to use the reverse pass; this is important for two reasons.   One, that in turning his back to the Black forwards he is less likely to be spoiled ; and two, he will be able to follow the movements of his fly-half during his pass.

# PASSING THE BALL FROM A LINE-OUT

*Plate 15*

The scrum-half has turned and is starting his reverse pass.

\*       \*       \*

*Plate 16*

The movement is progressing and the body swing is becoming apparent.

\*       \*       \*

*Plate 17*

The ball is midway to White fly-half. The back protection of White scrum-half is now apparent, and also the way that he has followed his fly-half's progress. On the extreme right of the plate Black wing forward can be seen coming up, but he has a long way to go.

# LINE-OUT IN DEFENCE

The following two plates show the use of the direct pass to the scrum-half from a line-out, in order to relieve pressure by a touch-kick from the fly-half as an alternative to the more difficult wheel.

*       *       *

*Plate 18*

This shows the scrum-half receiving the direct pass.   In this case he is using the normal right-to-left pass and has not reversed.   The reason is that being right-handed this is his strongest passing side, and the reverse would be more difficult and less accurate.

*       *       *

*Plate 19*

The ball is on the way to White fly-half.   He has remained perfectly still for two reasons.   One, he does not wish to become off balance or to spoil his angle of kick ;  and two, he has no wish to come any nearer the Black forwards than necessary.   He knows the length of pass and accuracy of his partner, and it will be noticed that he is already facing his objective.   As soon as the ball is received he will kick it over the forwards' heads to the near touchline, thus gaining some ten or fifteen yards.

THIS player is so important that I have devoted numerous plates to his activities.

His chief functions are dual: primarily to act as the first link of an outside chain whose duty it is to attack. In order to facilitate this attack the ball must be transferred at maximum speed, with a minimum waste of time, and at as great a length as possible, to the outside half. Only thus, so modern opinion avers, has the outside half, from the speed and length of the pass, a chance to defeat the open-side forward, the arch-villain of football to-day, and to open up the game.

In order to obtain this extra speed and length it has become fashionable for the scrum-half to cast himself through the air, landing approximately on his stomach. *Thus he completely sacrifices his mobility*, and the wing forward is allowed to make a bee-line for the fly-half, knowing full well that no breakaway *can* occur from the base of the scrum. This opinion and way of countering the defence I believe to be quite wrong, but it happens to be the easiest way for a scrum-half to learn at first to pass the ball, and so I have devoted a series of plates to the full-length pass.

Earlier on I said that the scrum-half's functions were dual. The first has been discussed, the second, which is just as important and almost totally neglected to-day, is of a *PERSONAL ATTACK* from the base of either the tight or loose scrum.

This form of attack necessitates two virtues: one, a critical eye on the activities of the open-side wing forward; and two, personal mobility, or *the art of passing the ball from the base of the scrum while remaining on one's feet during the whole process*. Thus a *PERSONAL ATTACK* can be launched at any moment from the base of the scrum instead of transferring the ball to the fly-half.

Should such an attack be successful a hole may be bored between the wing and the lock-forward, and a little simple combination with the nearest player, generally the wing or blind-side wing forward (cf. Operation Ginger), will result in a score.

But more important than that, even if the attack is partially stopped, it will result in the enemy wing forward—next time the ball is out—having to hesitate that momentary fraction of time that will enable the fly-half more comfortably to dispose of the ball or to make his own opening.

I am pre-supposing this hesitation of the open-side wing forward, as I am convinced that the lock-forward will seldom be able to get his head up in time to deal with a determined and well-timed breakaway. C. A. Kershaw (England), Mark Sugden (Ireland), B. C. Gadney (England), and Haydn Tanner (Wales) have shown some of us how this could be accomplished and how the whole enemy back row could be immobilised until the last possible moment by fear of this breakaway from the base of the scrum.

The art of whipping the ball away to the fly-half in one stride is more difficult to learn, and it follows as a training sequence after the full-length pass has been mastered, so I have placed it last for this reason. The value of the standing pass has been stressed because I feel that no one can be called a complete scrum-half without having it at his command.

The full-length or falling pass has, of course, its own peculiar value: in wet weather, when it is probably easier and more accurate; when the open-side wing forward has been recalled to his proper place and of a sudden more length is required; and under great forward pressure, where the rhythm of a falling body is not so easily disturbed as that of one standing.

But I am firmly convinced that the game can be kept open and therefore more attractive, not by curtailing the powers of the open-side forward, but by increasing the attacking powers of the scrum-half.

This needs skilful training, early training, and plenty of it. Hence I have tried in plates to show every movement of the standing pass, and at a mature age the well-trained scrum-half (in addition to giving his partner a quick and accurate service under all conditions) should be able to control much of the enemy back-row movements by the perpetual menace of this *PERSONAL ATTACK* from the base of his own scrum.


## THE FALLING PASS

### *Pass from Scrum-half's Right to Left*

The four plates which follow show the ball being passed from right to left from the base of an imaginary scrum, as in this diagram.

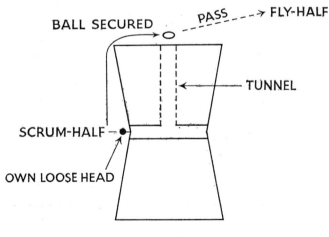

*Plate 20*  The ball has been secured.  Technical points :
    (*a*) Body and weight well over the ball.
    (*b*) Feet close together to allow the springy take-off.
    (*c*) Eyes on target.        (*d*) Ball firmly clasped.

*Plate 21*  The pass is being delivered.  Technical points :
    (*a*) The take-off has been made, the body being well clear of the ground.
    (*b*) The original drive has been made principally off the left leg.
    (*c*) Eyes on target.

*Plate 22*   This was taken a fraction of a second after Plate 21 and shows the ball going straight and fast.   The landing gear, his elbows, are coming down to take the weight off the rest of the body.

*Plate 23*   The finish of the pass.   Again a fraction of a second later.   The ball has now reached the fly-half, and this time both arms and legs are co-operating to save the body from the shock of impact.

The three plates which follow show the ball being passed from left to right, again from the base of an imaginary scrum, as shown in the following diagram.

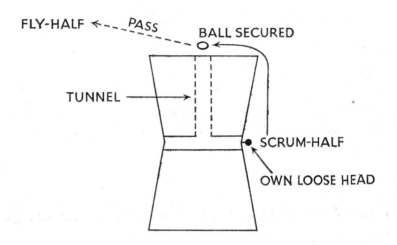

*Plate 24*

The ball has been secured. Technical points: the same four points as in Plate 20.

*     *     *

*Plate 25*

The pass is being delivered. Technical points: the same three as in Plate 21, but the camera this time has caught the scrum-half full in the middle of his dive, showing very clearly the perfect control of arms and legs.

*     *     *

*Plate 26*

The finish of the pass. Again arms and legs are acting as buffers and an excellent service has been provided for the fly-half. *But the scrum-half, as in Plate 23, is now temporarily out of the game until he can regain his feet.*

*Plate 27   England* v. *France*

J. O. NEWTON-THOMPSON (*Oxford University and England*), the English scrum-half, is using the falling pass from a loose scrum. Had he favoured the standing pass, he would have had the choice of passing or of the *PERSONAL ATTACK*, initiated by going through the large gap, indicated by the arrow, in the French defence. The English players are well positioned to support this "stealaway". As it is, by using the falling pass, he has forfeited the choice, and judging from the position of the French player to the right of the referee, his fly-half may find it difficult to start a threequarter attack.

## THE STANDING PASS

*Pass from Scrum-half's Right to Left*

The next eight plates show the scrum-half passing the ball from the base of the scrum and yet remaining on his feet.

This is the most difficult pass of all, and therefore the last to be attempted. It is the chef d'œuvre of the scrum-half, and it is seldom that a boy can do it really well, though it is essential for him to understand the movements and to try it out especially on firm ground. The photographs will show that on this occasion it has been done superlatively well.

\* \* \*

*Plate 28*  The ball has been secured.  Technical points:
> (*a*) The weight is entirely on the back foot, which is essential to the swing-through and to stop the ball being "ballooned".
> (*b*) Hands, back foot, and the ball close together.

*Plate 29*  The swing is beginning.  Technical points:
> (*a*) Head well over the ball.
> (*b*) Swing coming right across the body.  (*c*) Ball firmly grasped.

*Plate 30*   Mid-swing.   Technical points:
    (*a*) The weight is following the ball.
    (*b*) Eyes now on target.

*Plate 31*   The ball has been released.   Technical points:
    (*a*) The weight is in the process of being transferred to the front foot, following the ball.
    (*b*) From the hips upwards the body is parallel to the ground, ensuring a flat trajectory of the pass.   (*c*) Eyes still on target.

*Plate 32*

A back view of *Plate* 31. This has been included as it shows very clearly the shoulders parallel to the ground which is so important, and also the transference of weight from right to left foot. Notice also the straight arms and the head canting off to one side.

*Plate 33*  The beginning of the follow-through.  A beautiful shot, showing the power that has been put into the pass.  Technical points:
   (*a*) Weight now completely transferred to the front foot.
   (*b*) Body parallel.  (*c*) Eyes and arms to target.

*Plate 34*   The follow-through.   The best shot of them all, showing the perfect rhythm of the body.   Technical points: even at this last stage, when the ball was in the hands of the stand-off half, the eyes were still on the target, the body parallel, and the arms show very clearly that the ball has been delivered stomach high to his partner.

*Plate 35*   The finish: all the weight is now transferred.   Again the end of an excellent service to the fly-half, *but the scrum-half is still on his feet and in play as opposed to Plates 23 and 26.   This illustrates the outstanding value of the standing pass as opposed to the falling pass.*

*Plate 36   The Oxford Scrum-half in Action*

R. W. GREEN (*Oxford University*) and C. B. VAN RYNEVELD (*Oxford University and England*) in action.   R. W. Green, the Oxford scrum-half, feeding his partner C. B. Van Ryneveld from the base of a set scrum with a standing pass.   Compare Plate 30.

# THE REVERSE PASS

The scrum-half is passing the ball *away* from the side of the scrum into which he has put the ball. In the diagram the proximity of the touchline has forced him to use this pass in order that his partner may be able to attack.

Another use of the reverse pass which is shown later on in the book is to initiate an attack on the blind side of the scrum in midfield, thus securing the coveted position of "man over".

As there are two types of reverse, just as there are of the normal pass, I have included four plates of the *Standing Reverse* in slow motion in order to simplify the technique, and three of the *Falling Reverse* in action.

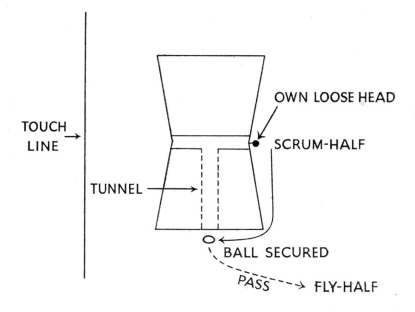

*Plate 37*

The ball has been secured. Technical points:

(*a*) Head well over the ball.

(*b*) Weight starting to be transferred. Note the right heel.

*Plate 38*

The swing-round is beginning. Technical points:

(*a*) The ball has been taken well back and well away from the body.

(*b*) Weight now nearly on front foot.

(*c*) Eyes to target.

*Plate 39*  The swing-round has finished.  Technical points :
(*a*) Shoulders parallel.  (*b*) Arms straight to target.

*Plate 40*  The follow-through.  Technical points :
(*a*) Arms still to target.
(*b*) Right knee bent so as to be able to obtain the full swing round.

*The Falling Reverse in Action*

*Plate 41*

The ball has been secured, the preliminary swing round finished. Like the standing reverse all the weight is now on the front foot. Eyes to target.

*Plate 42*

One second later. The pass is just about to be delivered. Note the strong drive off the left leg. Compare with Plate 44.

*Plate 43*

The finish. A beautifully timed photograph. The full swing round has occurred, and can be clearly seen from the angle of the body.

\*     \*     \*

*Plate 44   Harlequins v. Cardiff*

HAYDN TANNER (*Cardiff and Wales*) reversing from a tight scrum. The Harlequin forwards have carefully covered the flanks in case of the *PERSONAL ATTACK*, for which Tanner was famed, and this pause will ensure more room for the Cardiff fly-half.

\*　　　　\*　　　　\*

# THE LENGTH OF THE PASS

The two plates which follow show most clearly the supreme importance of the length of a scrum-half's pass to the whole theory of attack.

The first of these shots was taken by telescopic lens from the top of
the pavilion, the second from the touchline.

\*     \*     \*

*Plate 45*

Whites were on the attack. The corner flag can just be seen in the background. ( ↓ ) The scrum-half has delivered a lobbed pass of something between three and four yards from a scrum. His fly-half, who is just gathering, is, of dire necessity, running across the field in an effort to get away from the Black wing forward who is directly in front of him. This, in my experience, is the normal pass of a schoolboy of this age. If he gets away and manages to get rid of the ball, the attack will be going horizontally across the field with little, if any, chance of a break-through. Yet many attacks like this may be seen in first-class football, and even in Internationals, arousing our silent sympathy for the fly-half, who more likely than not is accused the next day of "running across the ground". At such moments we sigh for a Kershaw, a Sugden, a Gadney, or a Tanner. Bad training, bad for the players, and bad for the spectators, who are baulked of seeing the threequarters really on the move, because of the lack of a trained scrum-half.

*Plate 46*

White scrum-half has just delivered a pass from a scrum to his partner. The length of that pass is certainly ten and probably twelve yards. This can be seen by the positions of the halfway line and the ten-yard line on which the fly-half has his right foot. On the left of the plate can be seen the enemy wing forward and his threequarter line. If this attack does not develop, then the fly-half will be to blame, for he is already running straight and the amount of free space is obvious. The scrum-half (*ætat* thirteen) has just finished that essential body swing, which has made the length of this bullet-like pass. It can be seen from the position of the ball that there has been no "ballooning" in flight.

Here, then, is the key of the whole theory of attack, showing the vital importance of the long pass, and a justification of the space that I have devoted to the training of a scrum-half, who by virtue of the proper use of rhythmical body movement can produce a pass of this length.

# STEALAWAY BY THE SCRUM-HALF FROM THE BASE OF A SET SCRUM

I have called this a "stealaway" because it was not organised; it was merely suggested to the scrum-half that at an opportune moment in the game he might try a break on the open side of the scrum, preferably near the halfway line. Then we sat back and waited. The cameras were lucky. So, indeed, was the scrum-half, for he was assisted both by a slow hostile wing forward and the fact that the scrum happened to wheel.

No try was scored through this particular break, the final pass being delivered too early, as will be seen by experts, and the fly-half being tackled in possession.

\*          \*          \*

## Plate 47

The scrum has wheeled nicely and the heel has been clean. White scrum-half sees his chance—has made up his mind quickly (most important, and unfortunately not a universal quality). *Note the hands and foot close to the ball, the ideal picking-up position.* Black scrum-half is about to make a despairing dive.

\*          \*          \*

## Plate 48

His dive has failed. One of his boots can be seen on the left of the plate. White scrum-half is well off the mark; he has taken but one pace and is already looking for the gap. Vote of censure on Black wing forward who is only just getting his head up.

\*          \*          \*

## Plate 49

The break continues and now the gap is visible. White scrum-half is aiming for it between fly-half and wing forward. Note prone Black scrum-half.

*Plate 50*

He is through the gap—just.   Black full-back coming up to stop it.

\*     \*     \*

*Plate 51*

Another camera has taken over.   The final pass is being delivered to the fly-half, who has come up with his threequarters in support.   Black fly-half and wing forward can be seen on the ground marking the trail of the gap.

\*     \*     \*

*Plate 52*

A mistake in timing and White scrum-half seems to have realised it, as he is looking somewhat askance at the open space in front of him.   Had he gone on a yard or two he would have drawn the full-back on the left of the plate and his partner would have scored.   As it was, that player was tackled in possession.

THE halves constitute the major difficulty in making an efficient side. The scrum-half has been dealt with already at considerable length, and it must be obvious how much training has to be put in before the results of speed and length are obtained, and obtained they must be or all else is useless.

Let us then assume that the scrum-half has learnt his job. The next operation is to deliver the ball to the fly-half at the place where he would most like it, which is, presumably, as far from the nearest enemy (wing forward) as is possible. At this point we reach a controversy, rather an aged one, but even now none the less keen. Should the scrum-half always pass roughly to the same place, or should the fly-half be ready to vary his position in relation to the scrum-half's possible difficulties? Having been myself a scrum-half, I incline, with reservations, to the latter theory, as I have painful memories of a high wind at Twickenham, Douglas Bader missing my passes, and some acidulated comments by Adrian Stoop after the game.

Thus I feel that the fly-half, having more mobility and less present troubles, should be prepared to take the ball where the scrum-half can send it within a reasonable radius and not at any particularly prepared position. But wherever he takes it, it must be at *MAXIMUM CONTROLLED SPEED*, else his threequarter line will be reduced to impotency.

The words "*MAXIMUM CONTROLLED SPEED*" need some clarification. Unless the fly-half intends to go over himself from close range, he must *never* take the ball from his scrum-half running full out. The reason is that he has to pass the ball, and he should be able to pass that ball on in three paces from the moment that he receives it. This is impossible unless his body is in perfect control, and it is up to him to regulate his own efficient maximum speed. So often does one hear the parrot cry of "Take your pass flat out", which is an impossibility if you have to part with the ball quickly and accurately.

Having successfully mastered this—and I do not underestimate its difficulties—his job is to straighten his line. At the moment of receiving the ball he is, of necessity, running across the ground, and in order to counteract this he must take *a pace away from his nearest threequarter before he passes the ball*. Should he not do this, the threequarter line will be cramped together and if the ball reaches the wing that player will find himself in touch before he has even crossed the advantage line.

The training that makes a good pair of halves is simple—practice, practice, and more practice together, so that they develop a perfect understanding of each other's difficulties and know each other's weaknesses and strength. I always encourage halves to criticise each other's positional play and if anything is going wrong to try to get it right themselves by a little quick practice.

Besides the all-important job of link to the attacking threequarter line, the fly-half also has to do a certain amount of tactical kicking of either an offensive or defensive nature. That from the line-out has already been discussed; the rest will be dealt with later on in the book.

As an individual, your fly-half should have excellent hands, speed off the mark, a sense of body rhythm, an eye for half an opening—he rarely gets a chance of more—and a quick brain. Moreover he must he desperately keen on the game, be prepared to practice incessantly with his half, and learn, most painfully, to kick with both feet. In fact, he is somewhat of a rarity, as the history of Rugby football can confirm, but none the less to be sought after, and, if found, a source of great and abiding pleasure.

\*     \*     \*

# A CHANGE IN DIRECTION OF ATTACK BY A BACK-HANDED REVERSE PASS FROM A SET SCRUM

The idea is an abrupt change in the direction of attack from open to blind side in the hope that the fly-half will be able to get up and to draw the enemy wing, leaving his own wing to beat the full-back and score.

*Conditions:* Own ball and base of attack anywhere in midfield.

The two White centres on the open side.

In the following plates which show this movement in action the scrum-half has used an alternative to the normal reverse pass that has already been discussed.

For want of a better title I will call it the back-hand reverse pass. It is more unorthodox, and is greatly favoured by Welsh sides. It demands strength of wrist and arm as well as body rhythm and is therefore seldom attempted with success by boys. In this case my scrum-half mastered it and used it quite considerably with accuracy and success.

It is very difficult to describe in detail the movements of the body in the pass itself, so I have included two close-ups of a pass in order to make the technique more clear, before describing the actual action.

\*     \*     \*

*Plate 53    Close-up of Preliminary Movement*

The scrum has wheeled awkwardly this time for the scrum-half, but in spite of being half spoiled by Black scrum-half, he has managed to make the preliminary movement. The weight is on the back foot and this time will not be transferred, the ball being propelled by arms and wrists.

\*     \*     \*

*Plate 54    Close-up of Finish*

The finish of the pass. The scrum-half is looking out of the corner of his eyes at his target. Black blind-side wing forward is looking suitably impressed.

*Plate 55* Preliminary movement in action: White fly-half, having signalled his scrum-half, edges delicately a little more behind the scrum than he would normally stand. As the ball is coming out he must cross to the blind side of the scrum and take his pass, draw the Black wing, and give his own wing possession. White scrum-half coming round to collect the heel. Note good tunnel of lock-forward between whose feet the ball is rolling.

*Plate 56* The ball is being passed. White fly-half is now on his blind side with his wing outside him. His job is now to accelerate, draw Black wing, and put his own wing in a scoring position.

*Plate 57*

The finish of the pass in action.   White scrum-half is just about to be tackled by a wing forward.   Black scrum-half is on his feet again and is checking.   White scrum-half nicely balanced.

## CHANGE IN DIRECTION OF ATTACK BY A BACK-HANDED REVERSE PASS (*continued*)

*Plate 58*

White scrum-half has been tackled, but has already produced a pass both long and accurate that should enable his fly-half to force the opening. Black wing is coming up to deal with the situation if he can.

* * *

*Plate 59*

He cannot. White fly-half has drawn the wing and handed on a scoring pass to his own wing, who has a clear run in. Note Black full-back out of position.

# THE THREEQUARTERS

IF the halves constitute the major coaching difficulty of a XV, the three-quarters are the most difficult to keep under control.

Here lie your breaks through, your tries and your goals, your dropped passes, your tackle that gives the enemy his chance, your moments of ecstasy and of speechless fury. Young centres can play like angels or devils in the space of five minutes—they can look like complete novices at three o'clock and at five minutes past produce a movement that would have done credit to Wallace, Macpherson, and Ian Smith.

The reasons for this transformation? I think that there are two, one which can be remedied after much tribulation, and the other which if the coach is wise he will accept with philosophy, for it would be a poor game if one could control the whole of it from the touchline.

The first is a tendency to get out of position, and I am only dealing with the attack at this stage, so that the ball reaches the threequarter nearest the fly-half either too flat or too far back. In nearly every case it is the fault of the threequarter and *not* the fly-half, and the trouble lies in the regulation of their relative speeds. The threequarter tends to be up at the place of delivery either too early, thus finding himself trotting, or too late, and running flat out to get near the pass. In neither case is he at *HIS CONTROLLED MAXIMUM SPEED* at the critical moment, which is as essential to the threequarter as the fly-half. The only remedy to this evil as far as I know is the continued insistence on good positioning, and from the proper understanding by the offender that the damage was probably caused before the ball even reached the fly-half.

A certain amount of correctness of *angle* can be obtained by the centres aligning themselves with the corner flag wherever they are in the field. Naturally the further up in attack they are, the steeper will become the angle, and as they retire so it will get flatter, the angle being at its steepest when the scrum is on the enemy line and quite flat when the scrum is on their own. But this rough rule does not get rid of the difficulty of *spacing* between them. It is this faulty spacing, as well as the angle, that causes so many passes to be dropped and so many opportunities of being in a position of having to beat only the opposite man—and not his co-centre as well—to be missed.

And that brings me to my second point. It is here that the personal attacking flair must be allowed and encouraged to develop, and those responsible for coaching must watch their centres like hawks in order to spot the individual tendency that is most strong.

It may be natural for a boy to turn inside, to accelerate and round his man from the outside, or to go straight and hard through the gap that is there or imaginary. Whatever tendency he has must be strengthened by practice on the field and by discussion off it. He must be encouraged to try it out, and to think in terms of personal attack.

So on no account must he blindly and mechanically pass on the ball to his wing in deference to the opinion of most Rugger crowds.

This sterile form of attack must not be confused with that most rare of successful manœuvres, the lightning passing of the ball down the line, so that the wing is left with three or four yards in which to move, and use, presumably, his superior speed to round his opposite number and flash down the touchline.

Experience has convinced me that the wing is powerless unless an opening or half an opening has been carved for him by his centre. Macpherson did this for Ian Smith, and conversely the genius of Prince Obolensky suffered by having no equal genius playing inside to him.

To all centres I say : develop your individuality *at all costs* ; remember that the outside centre is more likely to make a break than his fellow nearer to the fly-half, and don't get discouraged when these attempts fail, even though the straight pass to the wing might have been a try. It would not have been so with the covering of a first-class side, and that, after all, is one's ultimate aim.


## DEFENCE

The technique of defence should logically be as complicated and varied as is the attack. But because few centres have more than one method of attack the defence problem becomes more simple.

The secret of a sound defence is the ability to come up quickly on to the enemy, thereby curtailing his attacking space and forcing him across the field away from the scrum. In order to counter this he will have either to cut inside, a most difficult manœuvre, or round his man with the aid of a hand-off, or best of all get rid of the ball to an uncomfortable co-centre or wing.

The procedure of the actual tackle is quick up to within striking distance—steady—and then in. Should the enemy be stopped before he crosses the advantage line, an imaginary one drawn across the field between the two packs, so much the better. But this is not always possible, especially if play is in midfield and both sides are lining back for attack.

The ideal position for the tackle in midfield is at the moment when the man with the ball, having been forced across, is going slightly away, thus presenting two very vulnerable knees which will buckle at the impact of a properly applied shoulder.

The technique of tackling has been dealt with later in this book, with plates showing the right and wrong way of procedure.

6                                    81

## THE USE OF THE "DUMMY" OR FEINT PASS—GOOD AND BAD SPACING IN THE THREEQUARTER LINE

The success of this form of personal attack depends on how realistic the seller of the "dummy" can make his pass. It must be tried at *exactly the same place* as the normal pass would have taken place, and the arms and head must go through *exactly the same motions* as they would ordinarily have done.

The head must be turned away from the defender and the arms at full stretch in order to complete the illusion. At the last second the ball is sharply withdrawn, and the attacker goes on, being careful to keep on the same track that he hopes he has cleared by his false pass. He therefore should be most careful not to swerve after he has taken the normal step away from his partner or he will lose the tunnel that he has created.

\* \* \*

*Plate 60    The "Dummy" and Good Spacing*

In the plate Black threequarter has used the dummy, though there was a perfectly good gap existing already.   Nevertheless he has bluffed the White wing, who is carefully covering his man and is on the wrong leg. Black threequarter spacing is good, the proper distance apart having been well maintained.

\*          \*          \*

*Plate 61   Faulty Spacing of the Threequarter Line*

Another action plate that shows most clearly one of the primary faults that ruin a threequarter line, which has already been discussed. This was taken during a school match, and the Black threequarter line is heavily to blame. The ball has been passed from the fly-half to the inside centre, who has safely gathered it. He is running across the field, but he has lots of room in which to move, so we will excuse him. The villain of the piece is his outside centre, who is crowding him. He should, of course, be midway between the inside centre and the wing. Had he been in the right place, a simple try should have resulted, as Black threequarter line already have a "man over".

These are the players who should finish off the break in the centre and score your copybook try, though heaven knows nowadays that the higher the class of Rugger one watches, the fewer seem the chances given to the wing. Hence the gradual dearth of great wings, owing to the fact that there are no great centres to carve out the opening that will give them their chances.

Those who expect a wing to score or even to make ground without this preliminary break often forget that this unfortunate player has only one flank along which to move, and thus is more easily vulnerable to the defence. He is comparable to the straight-moving castle in chess as opposed to the jinking knight. Unless he is given the ball with enough space to round his opposite number by superior speed, a movement that I discussed when dealing with the centres, or unless his opposite number is drawn out of position, he is powerless and it is merely a confession of weakness to give him the ball.

I remember watching the first 'Varsity match after this war, and seeing the two Oxford centres trying in vain to create this half opening for their wings. They failed, as many centres have before them and will after them, for the marking is as close in this game as any in the world, but they were right to try to do so, and I was amazed to hear a considerable number of enthusiasts, wearing a formidable collection of club ties, declaiming in no uncertain voice their stupidity in not getting the ball out to those impotent wings. The stupidity lay more in the stands than on the field. It would be interesting from a statistical point of view to know how many times in a season such giants as G. P. S. Macpherson, A. L. Gracie, and George Stephenson, to mention only three great centres, have been caught in possession, trying to carve out this half opening before delivering the ball to their wings. One will never know, but I am sure they would all agree that the proportion was comparatively large. The reader will realise that, according to plan, I am omitting the strategy of swift passing to the wing in expectation of that formidable weapon, when properly used, the Cross-kick.

Thus having, I hope, established my case that the wings depend almost entirely on their centres, we can proceed to discuss the abilities of the ideal wing.

First, he must be fast, and as a runner is generally of two varieties, either the antelope with the long legs and beautiful stride such as Prince Obolensky, or the lower geared stronger type of runner such as H. S. Sever.

Secondly, he must be taught to use every inch of turf allowed to him, and they are few, and he must be taught that the only hope of a wing, whatever the chance offered, is to go flat out for the line. He is the only player on the field who has seldom got to worry about parting with the ball, so he has *NO MAXIMUM CONTROLLED SPEED* but is full out from the time that he receives his pass. After that he can use any of the various methods of beating his man that are shown in the plates. Most of these methods apply equally to the other threequarters, but I have put them under the heading of the wing, as I thought that the near proximity of a touchline might make them clearer.

His defence is comparatively simple, being the reverse of his own attack, that of forcing his opposite number into touch, and being careful that a cut inside does not undo him.

Only one other point will I mention, and that is an historic memory of Obolensky, again in a 'Varsity match, hurling K. C. Fyfe into touch on the corner flag, *opposite* to his own wing. If his own wing is not in action, he may be able, with initiative and football sense, to come across and help the defence on the opposite side of the ground. This may touch on the ideal, but in any case he ought not to be entirely out of play, and I recommend that wings verge well into the centre of the ground if the attack has developed on the opposite flank.

\*    \*    \*

*Plate 62    A Great Wing in Action*

PRINCE OBOLENSKY (*Oxford University, Rosslyn Park, and England*) in full cry for the line.   Note the length of leg and the beautiful body control.   It was he who scored the two historic tries that beat the All Blacks in 1935.   He ranks as one of the great attacking wings of the game.

The ten plates which follow show the various methods that a three-quarter may use to beat his man.

\*     \*     \*

## THE  SIDE-STEP  OUTSIDE
*Plate 63*

The side-step outside.  The tackler has been beaten by a sharp side-step which has made him misjudge his distance.
Technical points:
(*a*)  The leg drive has been made off the inside of the right foot, while the left has been carried sideways.
(*b*)  The weight is being transferred to the left foot.
(*c*)  The ball is being held under the arm nearest the touchline to enable the attacking wing to hand-off if necessary.   In this shot it looks as if the hand-off *was* unnecessary, thereby taking off some of the speed of the break-through.

\*     \*     \*

*Plate 64*

The same manœuvre, this time not so well judged.  The hand-off *is* necessary.

*Plate 65*

The use of acceleration to make the defender misjudge his tackle.   This has been well carried out.

*       *       *

*Plate 66*

Again the wing has tried to use acceleration and the touchline to beat his man.   He has succeeded in the former and made the defender misjudge his tackle, but unfortunately the touchline has just beaten him.

# THE SIDE-STEP, INSIDE AND OUTSIDE

*Plate 67*

A side-step *inside*. The leg drive has already been made off the left leg, and all the weight has been transferred to the right. The defender is well beaten, though he has managed to get a touch. It will be noticed that the ball is being held on the side nearest to the defender. Although this is not technically correct because it precludes the use of a hand-off, it has one virtue in as much as it does not "telegraph" the player's intended movement.

\*            \*            \*

*Plate 68*

Again the side-step, this time *outside*, but with very little room in which to move. Note the proximity of the touchline. I have included this plate, as it shows the transference of the weight to the outside foot. The balance of the body, however, is not so good, though the defender has been beaten.

# THE HAND-OFF

*Plate 69*

The hand-off has been used. The target has been fairly hit with the palm, though perhaps the arm might have been straighter. The ideal hand-off necessitates a "turn away" and "lean away" of the body.

\*     \*     \*

*Plate 70*

Once more the hand-off. A better specimen than the last. There is more weight in the right place and there is more than a suspicion of the essential "turn away" and "lean away".

95

# THE BODY SWERVE

*Plate 71*

Here a body swerve has been used, as can be seen from the hips that have swung away from the defender at the last moment, making him miss badly. This time the ball is held correctly, but there has been no need for a hand-off.

\*         \*         \*

*Plate 72*

The wing has decided to try to beat his man by turning inside, a difficult manœuvre which requires excellent timing. To some extent bluff must be used until the last possible moment, and the change of direction made without "telegraphing".

It has not been particularly well done in this plate, the timing being at fault, the defender being only half beaten and the wing having to help himself with rather a desperate "shove-off" which has missed, as opposed to a firm hand-off.

But he has succeeded in half beating his opponent, though with better timing he would have beaten him completely. A certain amount of "telegraphing" has gone on, for the ball has been transferred to the other hand; it would have been better had he held it in both, relying on the sharp turn-in to beat his man.

7

# THE FULL-BACK

A PLAYER who is cast for this role has my sympathy, for during a considerable part of play he is, more likely than not, out of work. Yet he has to be ever alert, trying to anticipate every phase of the game. I remember after an England trial at Twickenham, a particularly easy afternoon for him, that I remarked to the late H. D. Freakes, one of the great full-backs whom I have seen, that he must feel fresh. I received the riposte that a game where the full-back has little to do is more tiring than one with plenty of work. The reason given was that the mental strain of anticipating what might and did not occur was far greater than the physical strain of action.

That indeed is the answer to the remarkable fact that full-backs such as Freakes himself, H. G. Owen-Smith, and Vivian Jenkins were seldom, if ever, seen to run. They always seemed to be in the direct path of the ball, and this was due to their uncanny anticipation of the possible run of the play.

Boys are unlikely to develop this gift to any great extent, but a good "fool's rule" is for the full-back to be opposite the ball at any given moment and farther away from it that he thinks necessary, as it is far easier to run forward than backward, a simple fact that is often overlooked. The general training of catching, kicking, and tackling has been explained in the plates that follow.

As usual the first two, after explanation, need practice, and that is all that can be done, provided that the candidate has good hands and a reasonably cool temperament. He must also be intelligent enough to know where the wind is, if any, and to vary his position accordingly.

The tackling is a difficulty, as I am of the opinion that the full-back will always be beaten by a player of any intelligence if he has room in which to move on both flanks. Should the full-back be able to force his opponent towards one touchline he has a reasonable chance of effecting a tackle, otherwise the odds are heavily against him, and the blame must be apportioned to those who allowed the original break-through. Coaches should applaud any successful tackle made by their full-back and, however agonising it is to see one's final defence pierced, should try to remember the peculiar difficulties of this player and sympathise with them.

As regards kicking, there are two primary rules only : (*a*) that the ball *must* go into touch, length being of minor importance ; and (*b*) that the foot must *finish on the target* in the same way as the racquet covers the shot or the bat hits "through" the ball. I also recommend that the ball is held straight, preferably with the lace uppermost, and that the toe and instep are kept well down. I have found that the lack of insistence on length is a very efficient remedy for "head up" which spoils so many full-backs, for it is the desire for the extra length that is generally responsible for this nursery fault.

The last and perhaps most unpleasant job of all is the stopping of forward rushes close to the line.   Here, the necessary technique having been learnt, it is a matter for pure courage, though it is of great help if it is suggested that the fall is *aggressive*, and designed not only to get hold of the ball, but also to knock the nearest forward off his feet.   Players dislike defensive measures as such, and are more inclined to fall properly and hard if they feel that they are attacking the enemy, and not merely acting as a sort of human bolster to a collection of ferocious forwards. Moreover, from a technical point of view, the aggressive fall is reasonably safe, the other fraught with danger.

Ideally the full-back should, of course, be able to kick accurately with both feet, but this is the final stage of training that may or may not be reached.   The same applies to widening the angle, when possible, of the kick, and to all types of spin and screw on the ball.

\*       \*       \*

*Plate 73    Fielding the Ball*

First position of a clean catch.    Technical points:
    (*a*) Arms cradled to receive ball.
    (*b*) Knees slightly bent to receive weight of ball.
    (*c*) Eyes on the ball.

*Plate 74   Fielding the Ball*

Final position.   Technical points:   (*a*) Ball well cradled to body.
(*b*) Knees bent as full shock of ball is taken.   (*c*) Head well over the ball.
     In both plates the full-back has turned slightly to the touchline.   If
he misses his catch or does not make a clean job of it, a knock-on is less
likely to result, as the ball will still be travelling forwards.

# RIGHT- AND LEFT-FOOT KICKS

*Plates 75–76   Wrong*

I have included plates of both right- and left-footed kicks which are technically wrong because I believe that it is the easiest way to correct the faults that are present in nearly every false kick.

Technical points:

(*a*) Body leaning back and weight away from the ball.

(*b*) The toe, and not the instep, of the foot has struck the ball.

(*c*) Reason for these two, loss of rhythm owing to "forcing the ball" and ignoring the follow-through which makes the length of the kick.   In neither case has the full-back made the nursery fault of "head up" or eyes off the ball.

\*      \*      \*

*Plates 77–78  Correct*

Technical points :

(*a*)  Body leaning forward and weight over the ball.

(*b*)  Heels off the ground.

(*c*)  Feet much higher, showing follow-through.

(*d*)  Poise of body, conspicuously absent in Plates 75–76.

The left-footed kick shown in Plate 78 is worthy of close attention, for it is difficult to find any fault in it whatever.   The balance is perfect, so

also is the follow-through, and the position of the right toe is particularly to be noticed. Finally the weight is well over the ball; in fact, the ideal kick. The plate is so near perfection that I must assure my readers that the ball was actually kicked. It was an absolute beauty, and bounced into the left-hand touchline as you look at the plate. From the position of the goal-posts it can be calculated what distance the ball travelled. This shows the standard that can be obtained if the right technique is followed.

*Plate 79   Positioning: Bad*

An instance of bad positioning by the full-back, who has left the attacking player too much room on either flank.   The result has been as one would expect.   The wing has taken advantage of this space to beat his man comfortably on the inside.

*Plate 80   Positioning: Good*

This time the full-back has positioned himself well.   He has *herded* the wing towards the touchline, and though he has partially missed his tackle owing to a despairing side-step, he has succeeded in forcing his opponent into touch.

# TACKLING: WRONG AND RIGHT

PLAYERS must realise that to tackle properly they must "go low" and that if they go low they will seldom hurt themselves. The chief difficulty I have found is to impress upon them that this is really true, for it is unnatural to believe that the harder one hurls oneself at someone, the less it will hurt. I believe that swimmers have the same difficulty in the first stages of diving in keeping their heads down. This is the point where it is essential for the boys to have blind confidence in what they are told, for I know of no other way of learning to tackle that is really effective. A suspended sack has some value, but it is not of the same consistency as a pair of bony knees.

When I am coaching I get the best all-round results by explaining the technique of going low, suggesting that after this has been learnt it is merely a matter of personal courage to make the first genuine effort, and that it finally becomes progressively easier.

The next step is practice of that technique in games, and although I have obtained the desired effect by a well-timed shout from the touch-line, one of the few occasions that a coach should give tongue in a game, there is little more that can be done beyond seeing that the efforts are sound, especially the position of the head.

The reader will see that the tackling plates are disappointing, and this weakness confirmed my view on the value of anything but practice in games. In a game all these boys tackle exceedingly well, and we were distressed that this could not be shown.

TECHNICAL POINTS

(1) Go low—aim always to hit your opponent behind the knees.

(2) Head behind the knees, and cradled into them.

(3) Drive into the opponent from the inside of the back foot. This can become a dive when necessary.

(4) The shoulder hits the opponent on the thighs and just above the knees.

(5) Time the tackle so that the whole weight of the body, through the shoulder, hits the opponent.

(6) The arms are brought sharply together around the legs at the moment of impact, snapping them together and drawing them closely into the body.

The next two plates show how not to tackle. I hesitated whether to include them or not, but as they embody practically every tackling fault that there is I decided that they were worth a close scrutiny. I may add that of all the shots that were taken the boys found these the most difficult, for cold-blooded tackling, and for that matter being tackled, is a fearsome performance if it is to be done properly.

This will account for the expression of pain and horror on the face of the wing, and I am sure that he will have the sympathy of all readers.

On each occasion he made matters more difficult for himself by stopping at the critical moment, which is why all these shots look like "stills", though in reality both boys were moving relatively fast at the moment of impact. I have included two more, which though by no means perfect are good enough to show most of the correct points.

*　　　*　　　*

*Plate 81*

A sideways tackle designed to force the wing into touch. Technical points :

(*a*) The tackle has been made too close.

(*b*) Hence the body and weight are not off the ground.

(*c*) The head should be behind.

(*d*) The shoulder is approximately in the right place, the knees have been hit, and that is the reason that the wing has been stopped and is buckling under the impact.

*Plate 82*

A tackle from behind and from one flank.   Technical points:
  (*a*) The timing is a little better.
  (*b*) Weight still on the ground.
  (*c*) Head again the wrong side.
  (*d*) Too high again, enabling the wing to withstand the shock.
  (*e*) The vulnerable knees have been ignored.

*Plate 83*

A flank tackle. The shoulder has hit the objective and this time the vulnerable knees have not been ignored. This is quite a good specimen.

*Plate 84*

A tackle from behind and from the defender's right flank. A much better example. Technical points:

(*a*) The drive has been made off the left leg, which has correctly forced the shoulder into the body.

(*b*) The head is on the correct side behind the other player.

(*c*) But still too high, aiming at immobile hips instead of vulnerable knees.

(*d*) Hence the wing is staggered and eventually brought down, but not cleanly and at once.

# FALLING ON THE BALL

*Plate 85    Incorrect*

The defending player has fallen with his face and body turned towards the enemy, leaving the ball exposed and open to the feet of the forwards, one of whom is dealing with him.  He is looking somewhat apprehensive, as well he may, for his body is also vulnerable, and forwards in a hurry are not the most delicate of creatures.  The enemy forward looks as if he is enjoying the situation in inverse proportion to the falling player!

\*          \*          \*

*Plate 86    Incorrect*

A better attempt, but the ball is still in play, though the body is in a less dangerous position.

CORRECT

*Plate 87*

Ball well cradled to body, shielding it from the forward, who is coming up full of aggression and good intentions.   The defender looks calm.

*Plate 88*

He has come up fast, and is tripping over the defender's body.

*Plate 89*

The defeat of the enemy, who is in the process of taking a first-class tumble over the body, leaving a triumphant and undamaged defender.

*Note to Plate 87.*   The R.U. rule on falling stresses the fact that the defender must attempt to get off or away *immediately*:  hence the defending player should technically in this plate be attempting to do this.   He was allowed to lie on it in order to get the position quite clear. In the other two plates he is well within his rights.   Referees, especially in school matches, should insist on a very strict interpretation of this rule, for not only does it tend to slow up the game, but many injuries can be caused if players are allowed to lie on the ball.

*Plate 90   An England Full-back Converting*

M. B. Hofmeyr (*Oxford University and England*) kicking a goal.   Note how all the rules of kicking have been faithfully observed, also the perfect balance of the whole body controlled by the outstretched arms.

# PLACING THE BALL AND KICKING THE GOAL

A MOST essential part of kicking the goal is the placing of the ball. *The kicker* must be careful to see:
  (*a*) That the mark is clear and facing the target.
  (*b*) That he has placed the ball directly over the mark.
*The placer of the ball* must be careful to see:
  (*a*) That he is lying at a right angle to the angle at which the kick will be taken.
  (*b*) That he puts the ball down at the angle which the kicker has already indicated.
  (*c*) That the "guiding hand", generally the one nearest the posts, is holding that angle (the "guiding hand" is lower on the ball than the "putting down" hand).
  (*d*) That the "putting down" hand does its job gently but firmly.
  (*e*) That having placed the ball down on the command "Now!" he withdraws his hands, preferably over his face, and does not interfere with the concentration of the kicker by moving about or having a look before the ball is kicked.

The normal angles of placing the ball are straight up in front of goal, with as little run up as possible, and a gradual sloping *away* of the ball to the posts as the angle and distance increase. It is generally fatal for a boy to tilt the ball backwards, as it tends to decrease the length and increases the margin of error.

The *kicker* must then see that:
  (*a*) The instep of the non-kicking foot comes up opposite and close to the mark.
  (*b*) That he keeps his head down and his eyes on the ball.
  (*c*) That his toe hits the ball at the base.
  (*d*) That his weight and head are over the ball.
  (*e*) That the foot follows through to the objective.

After reading these instructions it must be obvious that kicking a goal is very much a question of the accuracy of *both* placer and kicker. It is therefore most essential that they should practise together. The placer will then get to know the timing of his partner. Many kicks go wrong because of this lack of teamship.

# PLACING THE BALL AND KICKING THE GOAL

*Plate 91*

The ball has been correctly placed, and the body properly angled. In this plate the placer is using his left hand as the "guiding hand" and his right hand as the "placing hand".

\*　　\*　　\*

*Plate 92*

A try is being converted. The kicker has obeyed the rules of foot, weight, and balance. Note the left foot opposite the placer's body.

*Plate 93*

 A close-up of a bad kick that did not succeed. The left foot is too far back, the weight is not over the ball, the body thus is unbalanced, and the placer is moving his arms about with his feet in the air. He has also shut his eyes, which isn't very helpful. I must add, in order to spare the feelings of both, that this kick was deliberately ''laid on'' with as many obvious mistakes as possible.

*Plate 94*

A good one. Foot correctly placed, weight well over the ball, excellent follow-through, and good balance. This can be most clearly seen by comparing the positions of the left foot. Placer almost right, though he could not resist having a sly look at the result.

*Plate 95   An International Pass*

The photograph shows C. B. VAN RYNEVELD and L. B. CANNELL, the
Oxford and England centres, at passing practice.   The all-important
pace away that straightens up the line is most clearly shown.   Hands
and eyes to target, arms at full extent.   The vertical ball, the ideal
position for the receiver, puts the final hallmark on this pass.

# THE PASS: GIVING AND TAKING

Iᴛ is obvious that the giving and taking of a pass cleanly and accurately is of paramount importance, and that there are certain elementary rules that must be obeyed and untiringly practised. With a few exceptions, boys do not tend to pass the ball naturally, the chief difficulty lying in taking the pace away as the ball is being advanced. The length of arm inclines to curtail the swing, and the pass is short and jerky. They always operate better when passing from right to left, unless they are left-handed, when the converse is true. Hence, and perhaps rather naughtily, I generally put the best wing on the left.

At the beginning of a season it is a good thing to practise passing in a circle, facing at first inwards and then outwards, concentrating on the swing across the body, and finishing with arms at full stretch on the target and head over the ball.

Afterwards practise at the trot, for I defy any mortal to pass the ball correctly when walking. If you take the pace away there is not enough velocity to allow the ball to travel the right distance and at the right angle.

The technique at this stage is shown in the following five plates.

\* \* \*

*Plate 96*

First stage of the pass.

Technical points :
  (*a*) The ball is swung well across the body.
  (*b*) Hips are kept straight.
  (*c*) The outside elbow is kept well up.
  (*d*) Eyes on target.

\*　　　\*　　　\*

*Plate 97*

Showing the secondary stage of the pass, and the pace away from the receiver that draws the opponent and keeps the line straight.

Technical points :
  (*a*) This pace away is being taken.
  (*b*) The hips are still straight, thus keeping the feet in the proper direction.
  (*c*) The body is turning from the hips and leaning towards the receiver, thus keeping the rhythm of the pass.
  (*d*) Head well over the ball.
  (*e*) Eyes to target.

\*　　　\*　　　\*

*Plate 98*

The finish of the pass, taken a split second later.

Technical points :
  (*a*) Arms have straightened out.
  (*b*) Outstretched fingers show how the wrists have been used to give additional power.
  (*c*) The turn of the body is now pronounced as the follow-through of the pass is made, but the hips and feet are still straight.

Plate 99

*The giver*

Technical points:
   (a) The pace away has been taken.
   (b) The hips are reasonably straight.
   (c) The top part of the body is leaning in towards the receiver.
   (d) The outstretched fingers are again noticeable.
   (e) Eyes to target.
   (f) The arms are *not* straight enough to be perfect.

*The receiver*—an excellent position.

Technical points:
   (a) He is running straight.
   (b) Head and shoulders turned.
   (c) Arms ready for the pass.
   (d) Eyes on the ball.
   (e) Fingers widely extended.

*Plate 100*

The more difficult side from left to right.

Technical points:
(a) The pace away has *not* been taken.
(b) The hips have turned towards the receiver.
(c) The top part of the body has *not* leaned in.
(d) The fingers show that they have *not* been used to help propel the ball.
(e) Eyes are to target.
(f) The follow-through is very curtailed and the pass is going slightly behind the receiver, unlike Plate 99, where it is *slightly and correctly* in front.

In fact, a typical poor pass.

Both these passes were delivered by the left wing, but this is no excuse, for he had been through the same drill as the other threequarters. One never knows when one may have to go into the centre, and I hate to see a good player in one position look positively childish in another. In fact, it is a good plan sometimes to play out of your regular position in a practice game, for it increases your knowledge of the game as a whole, and the more you know of the difficulties of a centre, the more likely you

9

are to co-operate with intelligence. This does not apply to the half-backs, whose job is quite specialised, though there was a case some two seasons ago of a scrum-half who was, for some unknown reason, playing fly-half for his public school during the week and scrum-half for the Harlequins on Saturdays, an unnecessarily difficult task for anyone.

\*   \*   \*

# TIMING THE PASS

Another difficulty is to get the pass properly timed. In the flurry of attack players tend to pass too early, without drawing the man, to run across, or to pass too late.

In the early stages of training the following method is of value:

Flag-posts are set up in the position that the enemy threequarters would occupy. The ball is then passed from the scrum-half to the fly-half and thus down the line. The fly-half must pass the ball three yards before he reaches the post that represents his opposite number. This method of training impresses the need of drawing the man, of keeping the line straight by the pace away from the man to whom you pass, and the distance necessary between yourself and your opponent needed to pass the ball.

Three yards seems a great deal, but when this method is used on the run, instead of at the trot, as it can be by more deeply angling the posts, it is none too much when the forward movement of an opponent is taken into consideration.

\*      \*      \*

*Plate 101*

Scrum-half on the right has already transferred to fly-half, who is getting rid of the ball to the inside centre slightly too near the post that marks his opposite number.

\*　　　\*　　　\*

*Plate 102*

Inside centre has received from fly-half and is beginning to think of transferring. His flag can be seen on the right of the plate.

## FAST PASSING

*Plate 103*

A training method of promoting fast and accurate passing. There is no complicated apparatus in action, merely a couple of flags which are used as a kind of starting post. The object is to pass the ball as quickly and accurately as possible to the wing after the fly-half has gone through the posts.

It will be noticed in the plate that the ball is safely in the wing's hands at a comparatively short distance from the posts. On this occasion the dark-haired fly-half went through, he transferred to the centre in the middle of the plate, and thus to the wing. The two players forming the other wing were not in action. This method of fast passing is of particular value in warming up the threequarters before a game or a match.

# THROUGH THE "GAP" AND PASS!

A training method I have evolved that is of particular use early in the season. The idea was born from a book about the great Poulton Palmer, who, the author said, "was always seeing lanes in the enemy defence". Experience has taught me that many players find difficulty in seeing even the widest of lanes, and even if they do, and go through them, they generally do not part with the ball at the correct moment.

And so I "made" a lane consisting of some dozen very light clothes-horses. These had spikes attached to the legs, and being hinged in three it was possible not only to create a lane, but also to make it quite a twisty one.

The procedure is to set up the lane, move your threequarters into position, and nominate one to go through and to get rid of the ball *as soon as he has come out of it*. He will, of course, find the other three-quarters on either flank as he emerges.

The opposition threequarters come up on their man in the usual way, and are not allowed to turn till the lane is entered; but the player opposite to the one who is nominated has to run, not to the lane but half-way down one side of it before he is allowed to turn.

I have found by this method that a very realistic "break-through" can be made and invaluable practice obtained at backing up and exploiting a success by judgment of the final pass.

Any one of the threequarters, including the scrum-half, can be nominated, but, of course, the lane must be approximately opposite the nominated player, and it takes a good deal of practice to judge the point at which he will receive the ball and at the same time be opposite to the lane.

But I have been able to get all the threequarters with the exception of the wings through with comparative ease, and as this training is particularly valuable for midfield players I feel that the "lane" has justified itself.

The following three plates show the "lane" in action.

# THROUGH THE "GAP" AND PASS.

*Plate 104*

A simple example of the use of the "lane". Fly-half has gone through and elected to pass to his centre on the left. Not a very good pass incidentally. Black player who was marking White fly-half has correctly gone halfway down the lane and is turning.

\*          \*          \*

*Plate 105*

In full action. White centre has gone through and is transferring to his wing. Black centre marking him can be seen coming back from the lane, having gone halfway up it. The other threequarters have come up normally.

\*          \*          \*

*Plate 106*

This time the scrum-half was nominated. He is through and is passing to his partner. I would like to draw particular attention to this pass, for unlike Plate 104 he has obeyed all the rules, and a very fine specimen of a pass it is.

# TACTICAL KICKING

## ATTACK

THE following methods may be of some value in attack:

### (A) THE LONG DIAGONAL

Generally from the fly-half or inside centre, designed ideally to drop the ball into the wing's hands who is following up fast. I have never yet been privileged to see this occur, but it has its merits, for if reasonably well placed it does give the wing a chance of a lucky bounce or some footwork, and even if this should fail there is a chance of gaining ground by the touchline. The ball should be kicked high and placed well over the opposing wing's head. The best position for this kick is somewhere between the halfway line and the enemy twenty-five. This gives enough room for a margin of error from the kicker and the opposing three-quarters should be lined up fairly flat.

### (B) THE HIGH KICK DOWN THE CENTRE

Again from the fly-half or inside centre. The ball is punched high and straight from much the same position as the long diagonal. The kicker or some of his side should arrive at the ball at the same time as the full-back is trying to make his catch. More likely to be effective if sun or wind are hampering the full-back. Great accuracy must be used, else a good full-back will return with interest. A method much favoured by the South African side of which Benny Osler was captain and chief exponent.

### (C) THE CROSS-KICK

Generally from the wing who is blocked, into the centre of the field. Must be used only in full attack, as a bad cross-kick in one's own half offers limitless possibilities of the opposition opening a surprise attack. The ball is kicked across, as the name suggests, to the middle of the field. Back-row forwards especially should be coming up to take advantage of the switch of the attack. Once more great accuracy and a certain amount of luck are necessary for a successful performance.

## (D) THE KICK AHEAD

A tactical remedy against a threequarter line that is more concerned with defence than attack, and in consequence is lining flat up in order to tackle more quickly. A short kick ahead by fly-half or inside three-quarter, trying to pitch the ball between the enemy threequarters and the full-back, may pay immediate dividends, as they are all on the wrong foot. If it does not do so in the form of quick tries, it will eventually force the threequarter line to withdraw to its rightful defensive position, and allow room for the standard attacks of passing. I have often used it against sides which, finding themselves ten points or so down early in the game, have resorted to these sabotage tactics, hoping to keep the score down and to profit from mistakes made under the pressure of a defence that is only just onside. It has always given the required result.

For personal players, apart from this tactical situation, I regard the kick ahead as the last desperate extremity, the situation being that the player is quite sure that he cannot score himself, and sees no opportunity of passing on the ball with any advantage. Thus he short-punts ahead, hoping that the ball will elude opponents and bounce faithfully into his own hands.

## (E) THE DROP-KICK

This form of scoring points cannot be entirely omitted from any book on Rugby football, but I feel it must be approached with considerable caution by young players. It is generally a most personal virtue—you either can or you can't; apart from very general directions as to its obvious use, it must be left to the player himself to decide on its execution. In one particular season we had a fly-half who "could". In this case it was worth cultivating, so I laid on an operation in order to assist him. It was the usual one: scrum within range—own ball—code sign —straight back to fly-half, who takes the ball standing still—and over the bar. But although we had success and it was æsthetically pleasant to watch, I always regarded it more as a concession to the skill of an individual player rather than a serious form of general training. One certainly should not try to build one's victories on a series of drop-kicks.

Although I have described these attacking kicks and their merits, I must confess that I myself put little faith in them. It has always seemed to be a confession of weakness of attack deliberately to put the ball out of contact and at the mercy of both the ground and the elements, thereby sacrificing all personal control and initiative. Indeed, I would counsel their use only in the certain tactical conditions already described.

There are three ways of disposing of the ball obtained from the tight in defence.   One is to wheel and take, a method that I have already discussed, the second is to start an attack, and the third is to kick for touch.

The second is attractive, but there is a world of difference in the stamina of the Harlequins, who invented and perfected it, and of young boys who cannot run the length of the field with impunity.   So I have adopted method three as a means of regaining the attacking initiative.

The procedure is simple and, if faithfully followed, the results good. The ball is passed back to the fly-half, *who remains perfectly still.*   There are two reasons for this.   One, that if he remains where he is, he is farther away from roving wing forwards.   Two, that he is on balance and does not have to steady himself in order to kick to the nearest touch-line.   Both halves must know when this is put into force, and the fly-half will station himself at the most convenient place for his kick, the scrum-half seeing where this may be before the ball is put in.

Apart from the ground thus gained it also rests the forwards, and it is comforting for them to know that when they have heeled they will get this reward.

\*       \*       \*

# THE IMPORTANCE OF CHANGE OF DIRECTION IN ATTACK

THE positioning of the defence in modern football is so exact that it is becoming increasingly difficult to score from the stereotyped methods used in earlier days. From a tight scrum the threequarters have to contend not only with their opposite numbers but also with a cloud of fast and mobile forwards. In order to counteract this defence in depth, it is of the greatest importance to be able to switch the direction of the attack and catch the bulk of the opposition on the wrong foot. Various forms of kicking, cross, ahead, or diagonal, are constantly used to create this situation, but their weakness lies in the fact that the ball, once in the air, is out of control and much may depend on the luck of the bounce.

The sudden reverse pass or "scissors" lacks this weakness, but in nearly every case leads to the ball being passed back *towards* the defenders.

A more dangerous form of attack might come from *preconceived movements*, in which each of the principals knows exactly where to go and what to expect. American football is almost entirely based on these coded movements, and although these two games cannot, of course, be closely compared, there is sufficient similarity to warrant an investigation of their methods.

Intricate operations of this nature demand much practice and thus their conception and execution might lie more within the scope of schools and universities. But surely simple examples would be within the reach of any keen club side.

The following two " operations " are simple enough. Their basis is a preconceived change of direction in attack that will often bewilder the enemy for the short space of time needed to pierce his defence.

\*       \*       \*

OPERATION "SHORTS"

Evolved by watching American football, and being intrigued by the way they camouflage the man with the ball by their scrum, so that he can move freely on either flank for a short space of time under cover of the maul.

I thought it might be both instructive and repaying to try a similar movement, applying at the same time the principle of "man over".

Generally the least useful person in an attack on the *open side* is the blind-side wing forward, so I decided to withdraw this player and make my attack on the *blind side*, choosing as my base any place in the enemy twenty-five from which I could manœuvre two players on the blind side, as opposed to the enemy's one—the wing.

The briefing was as follows:

*Conditions:* Own ball, and the base of attack as already described.

*Preliminary movement:* Blind-side wing forward disengages with as little fuss as possible and stations himself four yards or so directly behind the scrum.

*Operation:* The ball is heeled. A direct pass to the wing forward, which is taken standing still. The reason for this apparent peculiarity was that, from considerable experiment, this short pass taken on the move was invariably knocked on. His job is then to round the scrum on the blind side at full pace, link up with his wing previously notified, and together defeat the hostile wing, nearly always on the wrong foot, and the full-back coming across.

Experience showed that the scrum-halves cancelled out, and that the only possible spoiler of this movement was the enemy blind-side forward.

But our own attacking player, by reason of four yards clear start to get moving, and the fact that he (*a*) knew where he was going, and (*b*) was able, if necessary, to swing wide of the scrum, could and did defeat this counter-measure by speed, even if his opponent had his head up in time. In nine cases out of ten he scored the try himself, and only occasionally was it necessary to transfer a final pass to the wing. But on one occasion, against a good side, when we decided to try it more than once (the first time was a try by the wing), we laid on a dummy instead of the final pass, and to our great joy and excitement it was well and truly "bought", and the wing forward went over.

The following four plates show "shorts" in action.

*Plate 107*

The short pass to the blind-side wing forward has just been given.  The scrum has inadvertently wheeled and the attacker has changed his position accordingly to get maximum protection, and because of this is taking it on the run.  For this reason the Black scrum-half is well out of range, but in any case he could not have interfered.  The Black wing can be seen beginning to come up to try to block the movement. There is no sign of the Black blind-side wing forward.  His head is still well down and, bar a dropped pass or knock-on, this is a certain try. White wing is just out of the plate on the left.

The next three plates were taken from the blind-side touchline.

*Plate 108*

The final pass is about to be delivered.   The White lock and open-side forwards have got their heads up, and Black wing is being drawn inwards, leaving a clear path for White left wing—still out of the picture.

\*         \*         \*

*Plate 109*

The final pass has just been delivered.   The wing has been drawn and White wing has a five-yard clear run-in.

\*         \*         \*

*Plate 110*

The dummy has been used instead of the final pass, as the Black blind-side wing forward has this time made an appearance and has gambled on an interception.   Had the pass been delivered, White wing might have been tackled by his opposite number, who has not quite been drawn. As it is, the dummy has been "bought" by both Black wing forward and wing, and the "seller", supported by the scrum-half on the inside, should be able to defeat the Black full-back.

# OPERATION "GINGER"

An organised breakaway by the scrum-half from the base of a tight scrum. Necessary conditions: midfield; own ball; the scrum wheeled; the wing and threequarters forewarned.

The ball is put in, on the loose-head side, heeled and held in the second row, the scrum is wheeled towards the open side. The ball is then released, secured, and the breakaway takes place *on the open side*.

The wheeling of the scrum, *if done quickly*, puts Black open-side wing forward out of place; thus the scrum-half has a gap between the opposing fly-half and wing forward. He concentrates on whipping through this gap, knowing that once through he will find his wing, who has previously come up level with the base of the scrum, on his flank to take a scoring pass.

The following three plates show this movement.

This operation was named "Ginger" because it had to be carried out at considerable speed in order to spreadeagle the enemy. We reckoned that twenty-five yards was good measure.

\*       \*       \*

*Plate 111*

The ball has been secured and the breakaway begun. The scrum has been wheeled and the open-side wing forward has been thrown out of position in consequence. This wheel can be plainly seen from the position of the halfway line. The White wing on the opposite side of the scrum, to whom the final pass is given, having been forewarned, is starting to get into position for the veer. Note he is onside.

*Plate 112*

Going through the gap. The ball is held under the arm, as no transfer will be made until the link-up with the wing, and the free arm may be used as a possible hand-off. Black wing forward seen on the ground has missed and White wing forward is trying to come up over his body.

\*     \*     \*

*Plate 113*

Through the gap and the final pass. Black wing is out of position, and White wing, in full stride, has no one to beat. Black full-back can be seen coming across on the extreme left of the plate. Black figures on the ground are, from left to right, fly-half and wing forward. On the extreme right is White wing forward trying to come up outside in case of accidents. The final pass has been nicely timed and the whole operation has taken place in twenty-five yards. The halfway line can be seen on the right of the plate.

An alternative to Plate 113 is a short scissor between fly-half and wing some ten yards before the full-back is reached in order to link up with the threequarters seen at the back of the plate, but this involves much practice and is generally unnecessary, as the defence has already been pierced by the original breakaway.

# THE MAGNETIC TRAINING BOARD

A METHOD of training that I have found most useful, especially in the working out of various operations in which some members of the side have special tasks and all must know what is occurring.

The board itself is made of magnetised metal and thus the thirty metal units, for want of a better word, will remain stuck fast in any position. The same sort of device was, I gather, used in the war for operations of a more serious nature.

\*     \*     \*

*Plate 114*

This shows the board itself, with the field set for play and sixteen forwards packing perfectly for once.

\*     \*     \*

*Plate 115*

The Author gives a little instruction to the half-backs before some practice. Note the deep concentration, so rarely found in other forms of school activities!

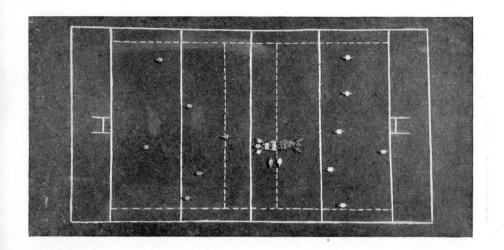

# THE GAME

RUGBY football is incomparable training for the character of boys. It engenders courage, confidence, a self-reliant aggression, and team spirit that is invaluable to them when they have grown up. They learn also to win with grace, and to lose with the same spirit: a much more difficult task. A good side must be first-class on and off the field. On it they must play all out to shatter their opponents—I do not belong to the school of thought which pretends that the result is of no importance—and off it they must be perfect hosts and perfect guests. Time and again I have seen these qualities develop in boys and over a considerable period it has left me in no doubt that this is a matchless game for the stimulation of these virtues. Moreover, it is obvious that they will be of greater value to the coming generation in these troubled years than ever before. In this light, I regard Rugby football as a most important part of a boy's education, just as important as the learning of various subjects in order to pass exams. The better they play it, the more they enjoy it, and in proportion the more these qualities are produced in them.

# THE COACH

IF I am right in the above valuation of the game for boys, it must be obvious that the men who teach this game must be very highly qualified, for should it not be properly taught its very virtues can quickly become vices. To be hurt while tackling in the wrong way, for instance, may easily instil fear and lack of confidence; it certainly will not do the opposite. Moreover, it is a truism that the better a XV plays, the more the players enjoy it. I have seen so many coaches who, with the best of intentions, seem to think that a powerful voice and a few well-chosen clichés, interspersed with suitable schoolboy expressions, are all the armament that is necessary to coach a side. I submit that this is far from being the case. It takes much hard work, argument, and technical knowledge as well as enthusiasm to get the required results, and by that I do not necessarily mean the winning of matches, but the playing of the boys to their maximum capacity of efficiency and therefore of enjoyment. It is important, also, to realise that this training cannot start too young and that the man who takes the lowest game is equally as important as the big noise at the top.

I would urge all those who are in charge of boys to take this trouble, and I can say with certainty that they will be mightily and quickly repaid.

# THE BOYS

THESE I have put last, for they are the most important.

It has been a maxim of mine for many years that good football is based on one word, "ATTACK".   I try to ram home to my boys that there is no such thing as defence in Rugger.   The tackle must be *aggressive*, aiming to teach the enemy that he had better part with the ball with all speed if he wishes to avoid being bumped.   The fall is *aggressive*, aiming to bump the opposing forward as well as checking the ball.   The relieving kick to touch is *aggressive*, as it aims to get the side in an attacking position.   When we score a try the skipper exhorts his side before the next kick-off to ATTACK.   If a try is scored against us, the fury is redoubled.   During last season our line was crossed but once by another school, and the player to blame had my entire sympathy, a feeling that the rest of the side did not seem to share!

So much for morale.

A watchful eye should be kept on kit, boots studded properly and kept clean, stockings up and not hanging round the legs, a peculiar fad of mine.   Only once did they fail me in the last item, and that was pure bad luck, as the scrum-half lost his bandage—I never allow elastic garters—at the beginning of a movement and had to carry on improperly dressed!

One more thing I used to do, and that was to write out individual reports, nicknamed "Dossiers", after every match for the threequarters and halves, which were kept in notebooks.   These were silently read by their owners at a meeting after each match and then interchanged so that each could compare their own strength and weakness—sometimes a source of much amusement.

We also had a selection committee, comprised of the captain, the vice-captain, and generally one other boy, plus myself and my colleague. The boys themselves, if necessary tactfully led, chose the side and gave the colours.   I cannot call to mind one instance when I have had to exert "presidential pressure", and I have learnt much from their own opinions.   That's what makes it so fascinating—there is always something new to learn.

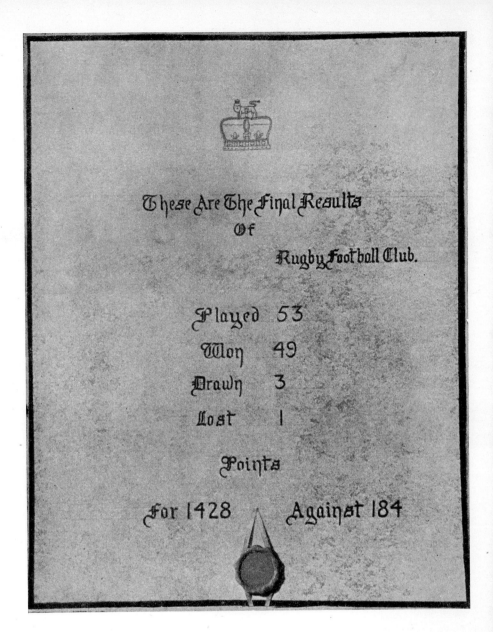

These Are The Final Results
Of
Rugby Football Club.

Played 53

Won 49

Drawn 3

Lost 1

Points

For 1428        Against 184

*Plate 116    Eight Years of Coaching*

This record was a surprise gift from my last Captain.   It was on parchment and he had done the whole thing himself.   I have blotted out the name of the school and the arms on the seal for obvious reasons.   I felt that from every point of view his gift would serve as a fitting end to this book.

# APPROACH TO ANGLING

*By E. Marshall-Hardy and N. Vaughan Olver*

This most informative book by E. Marshall-Hardy, Editor of *Angling*, and N. Vaughan Olver, an authority on sea-fishing, is specially written for those who wish to take up fishing with rod and line in either fresh or salt water but who have no idea how to go about it. It is of equal value to those who know something about one kind of angling and would like to take up another. It tells the would-be angler in simple language everything he could require to know about tackle necessaries and all the various methods of fishing. Throughout the text—which is divided into four sections, Bottom Fishing, Surface Fishing, Mid-water Fishing or Spinning, and Sea-Fishing—are clear, explanatory diagrams.

10/6 *net*